D1403805

DECLARATION

•

I hereby declare that
all the paper produced
by Cartiere del Garda S.p.A.
in its Riva del Garda mill
is manufactured completely
<u>Acid-free and Wood-free</u>

Dr. Alois Lueftinger
Managing Director and General Manager
Cartiere del Garda S.p.A.

Earth's Endangered Creatures

POLAR BEAR RESCUE

Written by
Jill Bailey

Illustrated by
John Green

STECK-VAUGHN
LIBRARY
A Division of Steck-Vaughn Company

Austin, Texas

*This series is concerned with the world's
endangered animals, the reasons why their numbers are
diminishing, and the efforts being made to save them
from extinction. The author has described these events
through the eyes of fictional characters. Although the
situations described are based on fact, the people and the
events described are fictitious.*

Editor: Andy Charman
Designer: Mike Jolley

Library of Congress Cataloging-in-Publication Data

Bailey, Jill.
Polar bear rescue / written by Jill Bailey;
illustrated by John Green.
p. cm. — (Save our species)
"A Templar book."
Includes index.
Summary: A biologist, a television broadcaster,
and an Inuit family observe the habits and habitat
of the polar bear.
ISBN 0-8114-2708-0
1. Polar bear—Juvenile fiction. [1. Polar bear—Fiction.]
I. Green, John, 1948- ill. II. Title. III. Series.
PZ10.3.B155Po   1991   90-44990
[Fic]—dc20   CIP AC

Color separations by Positive Colour Ltd
Maldon, Essex, Great Britain
Printed and bound by L.E.G.O., Vicenza, Italy

1 2 3 4 5 6 7 8 9 0 LE 94 93 92 91 90

CONTENTS

REALM OF THE POLAR BEAR

Anne-Marie Dupont pressed her nose to the helicopter window. They had left the trees behind, and were flying over a world of ice and snow. It was March; the dark Arctic winter was over. A weak yellow sun caught the frozen surface, making the ice gleam and sparkle. Gusts of wind whipped up the powdery snow into a miniature blizzard.

Anne-Marie had been studying grizzly bears for several years now, but this was her first chance to study the largest bear of all, the polar bear. She had come to help George Weinberg, another Canadian biologist, who was trying to count the polar bears on the remote islands of Canada's Northwest Territories.

Polar bears grow fat on a diet of seals in winter. The males can stand up to 11 feet high at the shoulder, and may weigh 1,500 pounds.

The helicopter followed the coast. The frozen sea was dusted with snow. Here and there massive blocks of ice had been crumpled and pushed into huge pressure ridges. Water gleamed in long, narrow cracks in the ice. George and Anne-Marie scanned the white expanse.

"Powerful sea currents never allow that water to freeze," said

In the far north, the sun sets for the last time in late November, and does not appear above the horizon until the following spring.

George. "These 'leads' of water are good places for seals, so polar bears come here to hunt. They spend the winter on the sea ice. It is the best time of year for hunting. Look, there's a bear."

The polar bear was almost invisible on the ice. Its white coat was certainly a wonderful camouflage. It was a fat, male bear with a thick coat, and his muscles seemed to flow along as he padded across the frozen sea. This was the animal they called "The King of the Arctic."

As she got used to the dazzling white landscape, Anne-Marie began to see more bears. They flew over a bear with two large cubs running after her.

"Those cubs look almost as big as their mother," remarked Anne-Marie.

"Polar bear cubs usually stay with their mother until they are at least two years old," said

---

The polar bear's coat blends with the snow and ice, allowing it to creep up on its prey unnoticed.

George. "It takes them a long time to learn how to hunt. To get at the seals in their breathing holes the bears may need to smash through that thick sea ice. Those cubs are probably not strong enough to do that yet, so they would have trouble surviving the winter alone."

The land began to rise.

"That's Southampton Island," said George, "our first stop. Many female polar bears make their winter dens here. We'll count the dens, and tag the females to see where they go in the summer. We need to know which groups of bears use which denning areas, so we can protect the most important areas."

A polar bear with her cub. Most polar bears have twins, but single cubs are not uncommon.

Above: *An expedition prepares for a journey across the Arctic sea ice. They have to take all the food and fuel they will need right from the beginning.*

Left: *A polar Inuit ties protective boots onto his husky's feet which can be cut by thawing ice.*

Right: *Snowmobiles are faster than a team of husky dogs and a sledge, but they can run out of fuel, and they have to rely on their driver to spot crevices in the ice.*

The helicopter landed near a small cabin at the foot of the cliffs. They unloaded their gear and made for the hut. Inside were two camp beds, a table, a lamp and some old packing cases that served as furniture. Anne-Marie lit the stove, and soon the smell of soup filled the cabin. George was busy outside.

"Supper's ready, come and eat," called Anne-Marie.

George came in, his cheeks pink from the cold. They had just finished the soup when there was a noise outside. As they got up to see what it was, there was a loud bang and a flash. George threw open the door just in time to see a large polar bear galloping away.

"I laid a trip-wire around the hut to set off the thunder-flash," he explained. "I was afraid the bears might smell the cooking."

The next morning, Anne-Marie and George set off in search of the dens. Snowmobiles carried them easily across the ice into a narrow valley. George pointed to the snow-clad hillsides.

"The bears like to den in deep snowdrifts," he said. "The snow insulates them from the cold. Here, they are also away from the big males hunting on the sea ice. Male polar bears will catch and eat small cubs if they can."

After a couple of hours, George suddenly stopped.

"Look up there," he said, and he pointed to a small, dark spot high up on the hillside. "A den!"

Anne-Marie and George left the snowmobiles halfway up the slope, so as not to disturb the bear, and cautiously climbed up to the den. George had a loaded gun ready in case the bear attacked them. There were paw marks around the entrance.

"Good," said George. "That means it's occupied. Let's wait until the bear emerges and see how many cubs she has."

They moved a safe distance away, downwind from the den so the bear would not smell them. They built a wall of snow blocks to hide behind, got out their binoculars and waited. The wall blocked the wind, but even so, it was cold, well below freezing.

After three miserable hours, a black nose appeared in the den entrance. A bear pushed her head out and sniffed the air. Slowly she pulled the rest of her body out, stiff after the long winter. She stretched, then rolled on her back and rubbed her body in the snow. She began to walk down the hill, slipping with every step, until she finally gave up and slid down on her belly, rolling

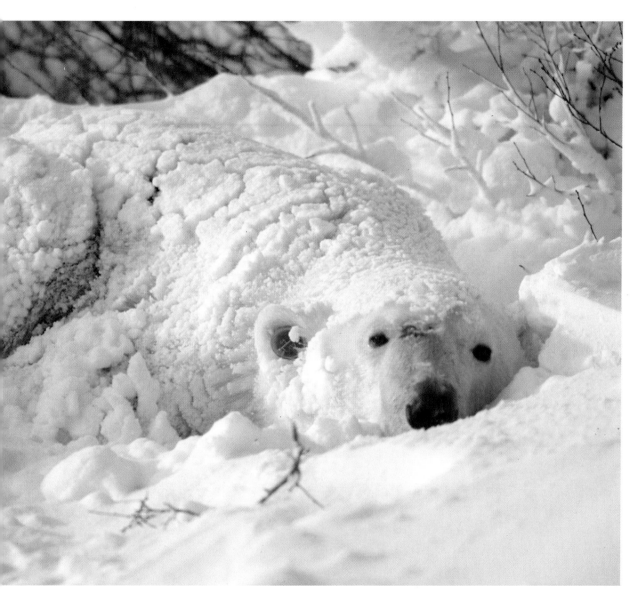

Polar bears get shelter from the wind in snow hollows. Snow on their fur also keeps out the wind.

Left: *The mother polar bear cannot go far from her cubs until they are strong enough to follow her. Rolling in the snow helps to keep her coat clean.*

and grunting as if she were thoroughly enjoying herself.

"She's got very long legs," whispered Anne-Marie.

"They look long since her belly is so thin," said George. "She has not eaten since she entered the den in October. She's been living on her fat and must be hungry."

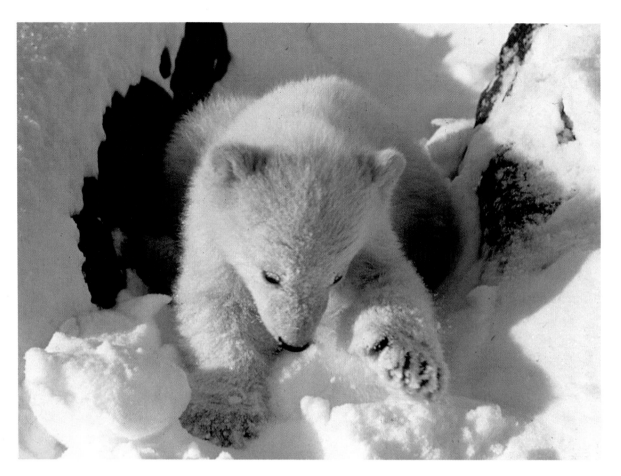

The polar bear was almost out of sight down the slope when Anne-Marie and George heard a high-pitched bleating sound. Two tiny cubs peered out of the den entrance. This was their first glimpse of the world outside. Gingerly, one cub put a paw forward to test the snow, then withdrew it, not sure what to

A polar bear cub takes his first look at the Arctic world.

make of it. Their mother came hurrying back, and led them for a short walk. Their tiny legs were wobbly, for they had not walked more than a few yards until now.

"They look quite big," whispered Anne-Marie.

"They are about two and a half months old," said George. "Newborn polar bear cubs are tiny, about the size of a large rat. They weigh only about 1 1/2 pounds, and are blind and deaf, with just a thin coat of fur. After about a month their eyes open, and about ten days later they can see. They start to walk when they are about seven weeks old."

After about half an hour the mother led her cubs back into the den, and Anne-Marie and George went back to the cabin.

About ten days later, on their way to visit some other dens, George and Anne-Marie saw the mother bear leading the cubs toward the sea ice.

"She must be very hungry now," commented George. "It's very dangerous for the cubs out on the ice, but their mother needs to start hunting seals again."

The mother polar bear needs to go onto the sea ice to hunt. It is dangerous here for the cubs. The large male bears may consider them a tasty meal.

"Let's go and look at the den," suggested George.

They wriggled inside the den. There was a narrow entrance tunnel about 3 yards long, which sloped up to the main chamber.

"Warm air rises," said George. "By sloping the tunnel, the bear makes sure the warm air inside does not escape. The Inuit use the same trick when building their snowhouses or igloos."

The main chamber was just big enough for a bear to turn around in. The ceiling of the chamber was covered in scratch marks.

"The bear likes to keep the snow above reasonably thin, so

The snow den provides a warm nursery for the cubs, who are born in the middle of winter. They feed on their mother's milk while she snoozes.

that air can get through," said George. "She also covers the cubs' droppings with snow to keep the floor clean."

"It's warm," said Anne-Marie.

"The bear's body heat is trapped by the snow," explained George. "The air in the den can be 35 degrees warmer than outside. Let's check the other dens."

The helicopter returned the following day and they flew to

the sea ice, where George wanted to tag some bears. When they spotted a female bear, the skilled pilot flew low beside her as she fled, until George could get close enough to fire a tranquilizing dart from his rifle. The bear started as the dart struck home, then galloped away.

Soon she was staggering, and within a few minutes she had collapsed on the ground in a deep sleep.

Polar bears' fur consists of two layers; long, stiff hairs for protection and a soft, woolly underfur for keeping warm.

Anne-Marie cradled the polar bear's massive head in her lap as George pulled out a small tooth. He wanted to count the growth rings on it to find the bear's age. Anne-Marie felt the hot breath on her hand as the bear slept.

Scientists weigh a tranquilized bear. It could weigh half a ton.

George injected an antibiotic to make sure the bleeding gum did not get infected. Then he measured the bear.

He beckoned to the pilot, who was keeping watch with his gun. The pilot ran to fetch a large canvas sling. Together they heaved the sleeping bear onto it, then secured the sling to the helicopter. The pilot started up the helicopter and lifted the bear off the ground. Then Anne-Marie could see the weighing scale attached to the helicopter.

The helicopter laid the bear carefully back on the ground, and George rolled her over so that she would be comfortable when she woke up. Then Anne-Marie helped him fix a radio collar around her neck and clip a plastic number tag in her ear.

"The collar is designed to fall off after about two years," said George. "The tag will help us to recognize her after that."

Suddenly the pilot shouted a warning. Anne-Marie looked up. There, behind George, only about 100 yards away, was a huge male polar bear.

While the bear slept, George and Anne-Marie fitted the radio collar. This would send out signals for about two years, allowing them to plot her movements.

"Don't move," whispered George, "and whatever you do, don't look him in the eye."

The propellers whirred as the pilot started up the helicopter. The bear jumped back, glared at the helicopter and then, as it came toward him, lumbered off.

"Let's finish quickly, before he comes back," said George.

He injected the bear with a chemical to wake her up, and they

Captured bears are often numbered. They can be identified easily when they are recaptured and changes in weight and height recorded.

got back into the helicopter.

"This is the bears' mating season," said George. "This bear has no cubs with her, so she is ready to mate again. In the autumn her radio signals will lead us to her denning area."

As they moved off, the large male appeared over the horizon. He was determined not to lose sight of the female.

"He may stay with her for several days," George continued.

"How did he find a mate in all this space?" asked Anne-Marie.

"In a female ready to mate," said George, "the urine has a special smell. Polar bears have a good sense of smell, and she will probably attract several males. They may even fight over her."

In the distance, they could see the great male was nuzzling the slowly awakening female.

In several weeks, George and his assistants tagged about 20 bears, and fitted radio collars to two more single females. It was time to move to their summer cabin on Devon Island.

The male bear is not put off by his mate's radio collar. The collars are so powerful that their signals can be picked up by satellites and followed hundreds of miles away.

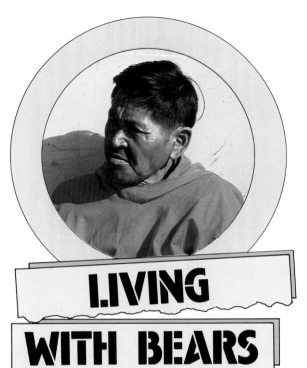

LIVING WITH BEARS

Sam Ipalook felt a tingle of excitement as the plane climbed over the trees around Churchill and headed north. His family had given up their nomadic life and settled in modern cabins in Churchill when he was a boy, but he still had the Inuit's instinctive love of the open spaces of the Arctic north. Sam worked for the Canadian Broadcasting Corporation (CBC) as a host and producer of radio programs, based in Churchill.

CBC thought that a feature on what the polar bears were doing during the summer would liven up their news broadcasts. Sam was going to join George and Anne-Marie, who were watching polar bears on Devon Island, far to the north.

As they crossed the sea ice surrounding Devon Island a strange sight loomed ahead. Steep islands of limestone rose above the flat, ice-covered ground, their sides rimmed with cliffs that dropped hundreds of yards to the beach below. This was a great place to watch polar bears. If people were on top of one of these rocky "islands" the bears could neither see nor smell them. The bears would continue to behave perfectly naturally.

They landed on the largest island, Caswall Tower, near the scientists' hut. Anne-Marie and George were sitting by the edge of the cliff scanning the land below with large telescopes. Sam went to join them.

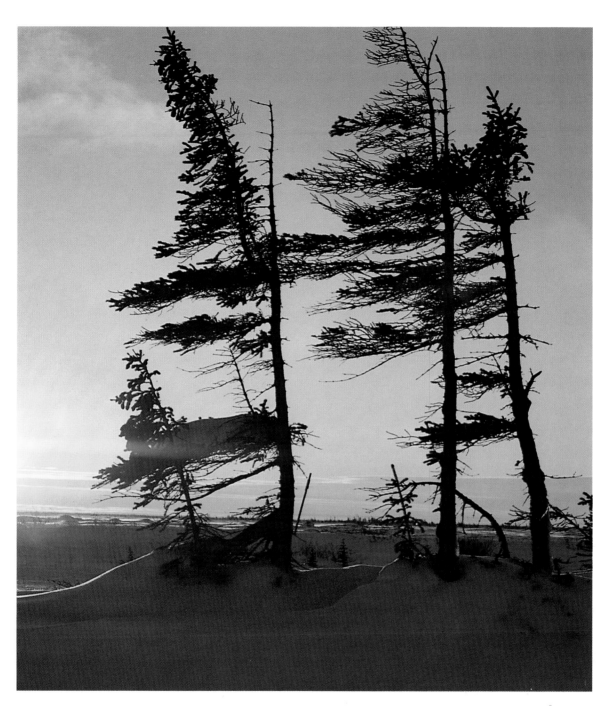

Left: *The ice was beginning to melt. Pools of water lay on the surface and cracks appeared. The bears were now hunting far out on the ice.*

Above: *These trees are often called "flags" because they have branches on one side only. The wind blows so hard that branches cannot grow on the windward side.*

Sam felt the magic of the ice all around him. He had forgotten what real silence was like. There was only the occasional creaking and cracking of ice as it broke away from the shore, and the calls of snow geese and terns as they flew overhead.

"The bears are busy today, Sam," said George. "Look."

The polar bear has fur on the soles of its feet to keep them from freezing on the ice. It has long sharp claws and very tough skin on its pads, which grip the slippery ice.

Sam settled himself down at a telescope. The ice was beginning to melt. Pools of water lay gleaming in the sun. The surface of the ice was wet and slippery. Seals were basking in the sun beside their breathing holes. He could see a large polar bear stalking a seal. It was creeping forward stealthily, like a cat stalking a bird. Every time the seal looked up the bear froze. When it got to within a few yards, it pounced in one huge leap. The seal was too quick for it though, and dived into the water.

"That must be an old seal," remarked Sam. "It has learned to react quickly. The young ones tend to freeze in horror when they see a polar bear."

"I'm surprised the seal doesn't see that black nose coming," laughed Anne-Marie.

"Seals are short-sighted," said Sam. "In fact, the bear has black skin all over, under its white fur. The black skin helps to keep it warm by absorbing heat."

The ringed seal is the polar bear's main source of food. The seals live on the sea ice, and hunt for food in the cold water below.

Later, Sam spotted a polar bear feeding on a baby seal.

"Where did that come from?" asked Anne-Marie.

"The seals give birth in dens under the ice," explained Sam. "The bears can smell them even through the ice, and they are strong enough to smash the ice to reach them."

"Studies show that the most successful way for a bear to hunt is to lie in wait at a breathing hole," said George. "Seals have very good hearing. They can hear anything walking on the ice

Ringed seals spend much of their time basking in the sunshine. They have to look out for bears.

above, so the bear must keep still. A tiny stream of bubbles rises to the surface just before the seal surfaces. This warns the bear to get ready to pounce."

"We used to hunt seals the same way," said Sam.

The following day they saw a mother with young cubs on the ice. The cubs were chasing each other and must have been alerting every seal in the area.

"Poor bear!" said Anne-Marie. "She won't catch a meal with all the noise they're making."

She was wrong. Later that day, the mother bear spotted a young male bear with a freshly killed seal. She was much larger than the male. As she charged toward him, he dropped his dinner and fled. The bear family settled down to feed. At first, they ate only the skin and blubber, or fat.

"If they get chased off by some other bear, at least they will have had the best bits," chuckled Sam.

When food is scarce, there is competition among bears. Young bears often lose their kill to older ones.

It was autumn before Sam had another opportunity to visit the bears. Or rather, the bears visited him. Churchill lies on the west coast of Hudson Bay, in Canada. Here, the sea ice freezes early, and polar bears from far and near come to Churchill to wait for the ice to freeze over.

In summer, when the sea ice melts, they are forced to come ashore, where there is very little food for them. They may catch an occasional duck, diving and taking it by surprise from below. They may also catch lemmings, tiny mice that live under the snow, but these aren't much for a large bear. Some bears even eat seaweed or berries. Most just lie around and sleep, living off their fat and saving their energy.

The town is a great temptation for the bears. Cooking smells and food scraps are very appealing to a hungry bear. Outlying cabins suffer most. The bears break through windows and even walls to get to the food, and most families keep a loaded gun ready. Fortunately, few bears are shot because the town has a bear patrol on duty day and night while the bears are in town.

Sam was to join the patrol to report on the invasion. Touring the outskirts of town in their vans, the patrol used firecrackers fired from long-range rifles to frighten away the bears.

Signs are put up around Churchill in autumn warning people to keep away from the area where the bears like to sleep.

When the sea ice melts, the seals hunt out at sea. The polar bears take to eating berries, seaweed, lichen, and even mushrooms.

The bears visit the garbage dump at Churchill for scraps of food. It is dangerous for both bears and people if they stay.

Sam joined the patrol at the garbage dump on the edge of town. Bears came here often, attracted by the smell. They rummaged through the dump, licking out cans and jars, and fighting over scraps.

The dump was also popular with tourists, an important source of income for Churchill. Tourists were watching the bears from a minibus, aiming their cameras out open windows.

Tourists visit Churchill to see the polar bears. This creates jobs and income for the residents of the town.

30

Some of the bears had large black numbers painted on them. They had also been tagged by Anne-Marie and George. The paint would be shed with the fur when the bears molted.

Suddenly, one of the bears reared up on its hind legs to peer inside the minibus, and tried to snatch a camera. The driver of the minibus sounded his horn loudly and sped off.

"That's number 27," said Douggie, the bear patrol chief. "He's a trouble-maker. He raided some cabins last week, so we picked him up and flew him 60 miles up the coast. I guess this time we'll just have to put him in the pound."

Later, they followed number 27 back to his sleeping hollow among the willow bushes. They set a trap nearby. This consisted of some seal meat inside a large metal drum. A trap door shuts the bear inside when it takes the meat. Once the bear was inside they would take him to the bear pound, where he would have to stay until the sea ice froze.

Some bears are such a nuisance that they have to be transported out of town by truck and then helicopter.

Anne-Marie and George were watching polar bears from a tundra buggy at Cape Churchill, about 40 miles from Churchill. Anne-Marie was surprised to see so many bears – they are usually solitary animals. Most of the bears were males. The pregnant females were already safe in their dens, and the mothers with cubs were too afraid to go there.

As she watched, two bears began to bite at each other's faces. They reared up on their hind legs and started to wrestle.

"Don't worry," said George, "they're just play wrestling. They won't hurt each other, even

Despite their great size and weight, polar bears can walk on ice too thin to support a human.

though one is bigger. They only really fight in the spring, when they are competing for females. Bears test their strength this way to learn who is strongest so they can avoid serious injury later."

Anne-Marie was thrilled. She had never seen this type of play.

Some bears saved their energy, and spent their time dozing in hollows they had scooped out of the snow among the willow bushes. Churchill needs its warning signs – it is easy to stumble over a sleeping bear that is covered with drifted snow, and bears do not like being disturbed.

By late October the ice was forming. As the ice thickened, impatient bears tested it, splaying out their legs to distribute their weight. Often they crashed through and swam sulkily back to shore. Eventually, the ice was thick enough to support the bears' weight and they left Churchill to hunt seals again.

Polar bears test their strength by play-fighting. Eventually, the weaker bear will run away. Neither is seriously hurt.

THE ARCTIC HUNTER

Inuterssuaq and his wife Elispee were just finishing the igloo when Sam Ipalook and the film crew arrived on snowmobiles. They were going to make a film about the old Inuit way of life. Here at Upavik, on the west coast of Greenland, a few families still lived in the traditional way, by hunting seals and other wild animals. Inuterssuaq did not depend on supermarkets and government hand-outs. He preferred to be independent.

The family usually lived in a small wooden hut. Occasionally Inuterssuaq would make an igloo if he was hunting far from home. He was making this igloo specially for the film. The husky dogs' barking announced the arrival of Sam and his friends.

Inuterssuaq had one modern luxury, a snowmobile for hunting in winter. In summer, when the ice was melting and cracks could appear almost anywhere, he preferred to use the dogs. Unlike the snowmobile, dogs could sense danger and avoid it.

Inuterssuaq was looking forward to taking the crew on a polar bear hunt – the highlight of his year. Families that live by hunting must have a license and are allowed to take two bears a year. Polar bear hunting is very special for the Inuit. An Inuit boy becomes a man the day he kills his first polar bear.

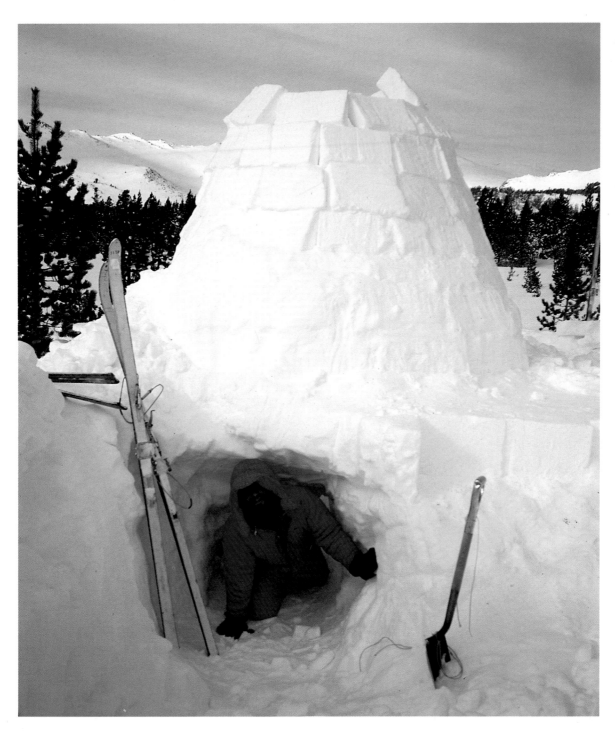

Left: *An Inuit fur trapper. Many Inuit still live by hunting. This man has caught a marten, an animal related to otters and badgers.*

Igloos are surprisingly warm inside. Few Inuit live in igloos today, but they sometimes build them as shelters while out hunting.

Sam had abandoned his town clothes for the traditional Inuit dress of a caribou fur anorak, sealskin boots, and polar bear fur trousers, just like Inuterssuaq's. These clothes would keep him warm out on the ice. Even in summer, a blizzard could blow up at any time. The bearskin trousers were his prized possession; it took a whole bear skin to make them, but they were wonderfully warm.

The dogs were straining impatiently at their leads. They had noticed the hunting preparations. Inuterssuaq produced a piece of polar bear fur, spat on it, then rubbed the runners of the sledge with it. Instantly, the thin film of water froze to form a slippery coating of ice.

They set off under a blue sky and brilliant sun, racing over the ice toward the hazy horizon. Seals plopped into the water as they approached. Inuterssuaq talked about the polar bears.

"We use almost all parts of the bear," he said, "the skins for clothes, the meat for the dogs. Polar bears suffer badly from worms, and these can infect humans, too, so we don't eat their meat ourselves. If we don't need

The equipment was loaded onto three wooden sleds. Each would be pulled by a team of up to ten dogs. It was some time before they were ready to go.

the skin, we sell it – it fetches about $200 a foot, measuring from head to tail."

After about 6 miles, Inuterssuaq stopped and got out a long telescope to scan the horizon for polar bears.

Although the Inuit traditionally wear clothes of real fur, researchers and explorers wear polar suits of synthetic fibers which are just as good at keeping out the cold.

Sam asked Inuterssuaq how far the bears roamed.

"The polar Inuit name for the polar bear is 'pisugtooq', which means 'the great wanderer'," replied Inuterssuaq. "Most bears don't travel more than about 60 miles from their place of birth, but some of the bears of east Greenland regularly cross the ice to Svalbard, off the north coast of Norway, 1,800 miles away."

"I didn't know they lived in Norway," said the cameraman.

"People think once they even lived in southern Norway, and in southern Alaska, too," said Inuterssuaq, "but hunters killed all the bears there. Today they still live in the Soviet Union, Svalbard, Greenland, Canada, and Alaska. There are about 12 distinct

The Inuit have always hunted polar bears, but they take only as many as they need. Polar bears and Inuit have lived and survived together for thousands of years.

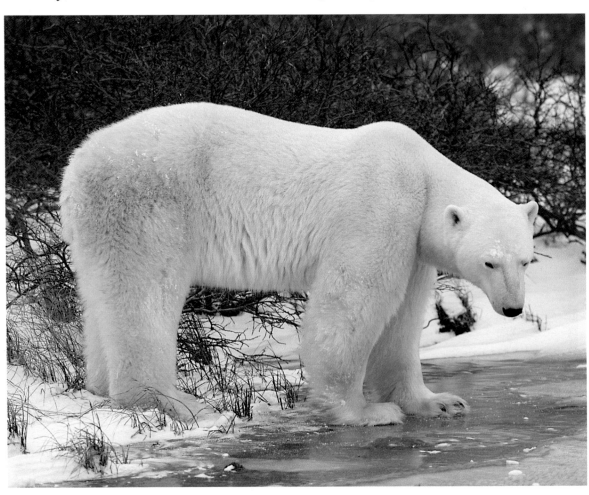

populations in 8 million square miles of snow and ice."

"Did Indian hunters kill off the southern bears?" asked one of the camermen.

"No," replied Sam. "It was the Europeans. First they came for the whales. Then, when there were no whales left, they hunted the seals until they, too, began to decline. So they started on the bears, not killing them for food but for the skins, to sell them in Europe, and just for 'sport'.

Then in the 1940s hunters began to come in by the plane-load. Mostly rich Americans. They even chased the bears in planes."

Inuterssuaq turned the sledge to the west, and soon the cries of gulls led them to traces of a polar bear kill.

Polar bears are good swimmers. They swim with a "dog-paddle" stroke, head stretched forward. They have been seen swimming over 180 miles from land.

A messy seal carcass lay on the ice, and an Arctic fox scampered away as they approached.

"How do the bears keep their fur so white?" asked Sam.

"They roll in the snow to clean themselves after eating," said Inuterssuaq. "They also lick their fur, and perhaps even wash if there is water nearby."

"Did you notice the fox?" asked Inuterssuaq. "They survive the winter here almost entirely by feeding on the remains of polar bear kills. Each fox follows its own polar bear, waiting for a kill. The bears get annoyed with them, but the foxes are too quick for them to do much about it."

They followed the bear's tracks in the snow.

"This is a male bear," said Inuterssuaq. "His footprints are about three times larger than the female's, but then he is about three times bigger than she is."

Now they could see the bear in the distance. It had already gotten wind of them. It stood stock still, one paw raised in the air. Then it reared up on its hind legs and sniffed the air, snorting in annoyance.

The film crew had their cameras ready. Inuterssuaq unleashed the dogs, who charged

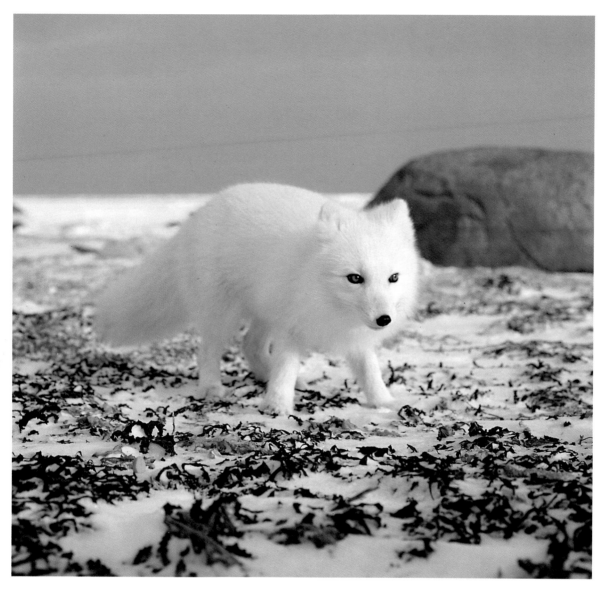

toward the bear. At first the bear stood its ground. Then, as the dogs got closer, it slowly backed away. Inuterssuaq raised his rifle.

Arctic foxes are a familiar sight wherever there are bears. They follow the bears hoping to snatch a scrap of food.

Left: *Polar bears have a powerful sense of smell. They often stand on their hind legs to sniff the air, and to get a better view.*

Suddenly, the bear slipped sideways into a lead of dark water they had not noticed, and swam quietly away.

"It's getting too late to chase another bear," said Inuterssuaq. "We shall have to try again tomorrow."

They sat down to enjoy steaming mugs of coffee before returning to the village. Sam was enthralled by the beauty of the scene, and the incredible silence.

"I had forgotten how quiet the Arctic could be," he said.

"It's not so quiet these days," said Inuterssuaq. "There are oil exploration rigs, ice-breakers, and planes. There are too many people here; one day there will be a big disaster, you will see. If one of those oil rigs leaks, the oil will spread for a great distance under the ice, and that is where the shrimps live that the fish feed on. The seals eat the fish, and the bears eat the seals – in time they will all suffer."

"There's an even bigger threat," said Sam. "It's called the 'greenhouse effect'. All the gases industry is putting into the atmosphere, the burning of gasoline by cars, and the carbon dioxide from the burning of the rain forests, are causing the planet to warm up. Already parts of the Arctic ice sheet have thinned by one third. If it melts, the polar bear will lose vast areas of its home. Unless we can stop this pollution, that beautiful sun we are watching may destroy the world of the polar bear."

Left: *An oil rig in the Arctic Sea. Increased industry means more people and this means that wildlife is disturbed. People and bears are meeting more and more often.*

It is too soon to say that the polar bear has been saved from extinction but for the moment, it is still "The King of the Arctic."

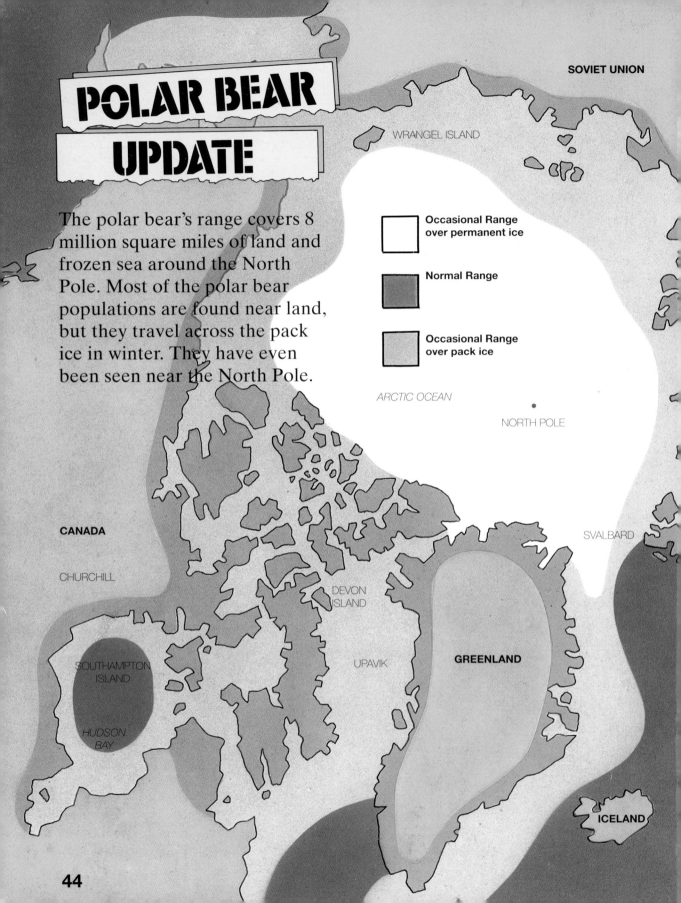

POLAR BEAR UPDATE

The polar bear's range covers 8 million square miles of land and frozen sea around the North Pole. Most of the polar bear populations are found near land, but they travel across the pack ice in winter. They have even been seen near the North Pole.

SOVIET UNION

WRANGEL ISLAND

☐ Occasional Range over permanent ice

■ Normal Range

☐ Occasional Range over pack ice

ARCTIC OCEAN

NORTH POLE

CANADA

SVALBARD

CHURCHILL

DEVON ISLAND

SOUTHAMPTON ISLAND

UPAVIK

GREENLAND

HUDSON BAY

ICELAND

A Conservation Success Story

Soon after the Europeans arrived in the Arctic, they began to hunt and slaughter the large animals that lived there. First they hunted whales, then seals, and finally, polar bears.

In the 1960s, the Soviets became worried about the slaughter. They had banned the hunting of polar bears in the Soviet Union in the 1950s. *The New York Times* also ran a feature on the unsporting slaughter of polar bears. The five polar nations – the United States, Canada, Denmark (which governs Greenland), Norway, and the Soviet Union – got together to make plans to study the polar bears, and in 1973 they signed an agreement to protect the bears. The International Union for the Conservation of Nature and Natural Resources (IUCN) set up a special research group to advise on managing the bears. It was thought that there might be only 5,000–10,000 polar bears left in the entire world.

• In most countries today, hunting of polar bears is banned, except by native people, such as the Inuit, who live by hunting. In recent years, guns have made these people's hunting much more successful. Now they are only allowed to hunt a certain number of bears. This ensures that the bear population is not seriously affected. They are not allowed to hunt during the time of year when female bears are pregnant and they are forbidden to shoot females with cubs. Since these rules were set up the polar bear population has increased to 20,000–40,000.

• Some countries have set aside special reserves where polar bears are completely protected. Canada has its Polar Bear Pass, a popular migration route for the bears, Denmark has the East Greenland National Park, and the Soviet Union has Wrangel Island, off the coast of Siberia.

• The most important remaining threat to the bears is the warming of the planet due to the "greenhouse effect". It will be much harder to introduce worldwide pollution controls to keep the polar ice sheets from melting.

INDEX

Picture credits
(*a*=above, *m*=middle, *b*=below, *r*=right, *l*=left)

Cover: *Portraits: a* The Hutchison Library;
m P.W. Bading/Zefa Picture Library;
b John Lythgoe/Planet Earth Pictures
Polar Bear: Leonard Lee Rue III/Bruce Coleman Ltd.

Page 5 Fred Bruemmer; *page 6* The Hutchison Library;
page 7 M. Macri/Frank Lane Picture Agency; *page 8* Thor
Larsen/Bruce Coleman Ltd; *page 9* John E. Swedberg/
Ardea; *page 10 a* M. Macri/Frank Lane Picture Agency,
b B and C Alexander/Bruce Coleman Ltd; *page 13* Planet
Earth Pictures; *page 14* Thor Larsen/Bruce Coleman Ltd;
page 17 Dan Guravich/WWF; *page 18* B and C
Alexander/Bruce Coleman Ltd; *page 20* Fred Bruemmer;
page 22 a P.W. Bading/Zefa Picture Library, *b* Jim
Brandenburg/Planet Earth Pictures; *page 23* Fred
Bruemmer; *page 24* Leonard Lee Rue III/Bruce Coleman Ltd;
page 26 Eric and David Hosking; *page 29 a and b* Leonard
Lee Rue III/Bruce Coleman Ltd; *page 30* Mark Newman/
Frank Lane Picture Agency; *page 32* Leonard Lee Rue III/
Bruce Coleman Ltd; *page 34 a* John Lythgoe/Planet Earth
Pictures, *b* Nicholas Devore/Bruce Coleman Ltd; *page 35*
Mark Newman/Frank Lane Picture Agency; *page 37* Fred
Bruemmer; *page 38* Leonard Lee Rue III/ Bruce Coleman Ltd;
page 39 Ian Beames/Ardea; *page 41* Wayne Lankinen/
Bruce Coleman Ltd; *page 42 and 43* Fred Bruemmer.

Map illustration by Ron Wooldridge.

A Templar Book
Devised and produced by The Templar Company plc
Pippbrook Mill, London Road, Dorking
Surrey RH4 1JE, Great Britain
Copyright © 1991 by The Templar Company plc
Original text, design and illustrations copyright © 1991 by
The Templar Company plc